CLEAR SENSE

CLEAR SENSE

Stories By

Ninamaste MaTuri

I give big thanks to my family and friends for their love and support from the start to finish of this book.

Contents

Desiring

Melanie

Chapter One

Bush's "Swallowed" played on the stereo in the dimly lit basement. Swirls of heavy white smoke hung in the room.

"Rome is in town. You guys will get a chance to meet him," Karen said as she inhaled a joint pinched between her fingers. Her blue eyes rolled up as her eyelids closed slowly upon them. Smoke prickled her throat as it traveled to her stomach. She held the smoke there for a moment then released it through her nose.

Karen's feet rested on a coffee table in her parents' basement. She opened her eyes and blankly stared at her toes. She began to wiggle them. She erupted in laughter at the sight of the movement of her toes. "Look at them piggies move!" she managed to say in between her laughter.

She turned to look at her cousin, Keith, who was staring back at her with glazed eyes. He wasn't laughing. "Looks like someone needs a little more of this," Karen said and passed him the joint.

"I can't wait to see your mom's face when you bring a black dude home," Keith said in a dull voice. He lightly twirled a lock of his blonde hair in one hand with the joint in the other.

"They have to be around to meet him first," Karen said nonchalantly.

Keith took a hit of the joint and attempted to pass it to his other cousin Melanie, but she smacked his hand away from her. The weed flew from Keith's hand to the Berber carpeted floor.

"Don't pass that shit to me!" Melanie shouted.

"Save the ganja!" Karen yelped as she rolled off the couch. She crawled to the joint, picked it up, and took a hit.

"Damn, cuz. I was just trying to share the love," Keith said. His head hung lazily to his right side. He fell back into the couch and began singing with Gavin Rossdale, "Just wanted to be myself."

Melanie shook her head as she continued to finish a drawing in her sketchpad. Her brown eyes were focused as her light brown hand slid across the page. Karen crawled over to the club chair where Melanie sat. She lifted herself up and sat on the arm of the chair as she continued to smoke. Karen looked at the drawing.

"Hmm. If only Tiffany knew her number one fan is sitting right here," Karen said.

"More like number one stalker," Keith quipped. "Damn Karen. Puff, puff, pass."

"Here, girly-boy!" She reached over Melanie and handed the roach to Keith.

"Are you fucking kidding me? Your greedy ass smoked the whole thing!" Keith exclaimed as he looked disgustedly at the roach.

"Not the whole thing," Karen said. She got off the chair, removed tweezers from her purse that were resting on the coffee table, and handed them to Keith. Keith pinched the roach and finished it off.

"Done," Melanie said as she stood up and proudly looked at the drawing. Keith and Karen stood on either side of Melanie.

"Wow. It looks just like her. She seems to be glowing," Keith said.

"She is beautiful," Melanie said.

Melanie remembered the inspiration for the drawing. The weather last week was the warmest it had been so far this spring. Kansas City, Missouri, had experienced a long winter and everybody seemed to have a severe case of cabin fever as they burst from their homes into the warm air. Pale skin and light-deprived eyes swarmed the streets. From the Power and Light district to barbeque restaurants to the parks, people were everywhere.

Melanie sat at the edge of the J. C. Nichols Memorial fountain. She was drawing one of the fountain's equestrian figures when her eyes caught something dark slowly moving towards her. Melanie soon recognized it was Tiffany, a girl she went to high school with. Melanie's breathing had slowed as she'd taken in Tiffany's Halle Berry-styled haircut and black shiny eyes. Melanie was captivated. Tiffany had walked past Melanie. Melanie's eyes followed her as she walked to her boyfriend, Michael. She watched the two hug. Tiffany's face glowed from the embrace and Melanie, doing what she often did at times like this, took a mental picture.

Melanie snapped back to the present moment and asked, "Are you guys ready to go?"

"Yeah, but I need to eat first," Karen replied.

Karen grabbed her purse as Melanie carefully removed the drawing from the sketchpad. Melanie, Karen, and Keith left the house and climbed into Karen's car. Melanie felt Karen staring at her from the front passenger seat. She turned to see watery blue eyes looking at her.

"Melanie. Has anyone told you that you look like a juicy cheeseburger?" Karen asked then laughed.

Keith began to laugh hysterically at Karen's question from the back seat.

"A cheeseburger with an afro!" Keith shouted. Keith and Karen laughed.

Melanie chuckled as she started the car and pulled out of the driveway.

"Let's make this quick," Melanie said, as they walked into a gas station. Karen and Keith headed to the snack aisle. Melanie walked over to the magazine stand and thumbed through a few pages of *Motorcycle* magazine. She admired the bikes she saw on the pages. The sight of the smooth and muscular metal made her heart skip a few beats. She heard her cousins making their way to the front of the store. Melanie brought the magazine to the counter.

"Hey, Karen, what does this remind you of?" Keith asked. He grabbed a purple-haired lucky troll doll from a display case on the counter and ripped its head off.

"My Barbies. You bastard. I can't believe you killed my Barbies!" Karen yelled.

Keith smirked.

"Hey, you kids are gonna have to pay for that!" the clerk shouted.

"Put it on my tab," Keith said to the clerk.

Melanie ignored the twosome as they bickered about the time Keith beheaded Karen's Barbies on a Christmas day back when they were younger. He'd then tossed the heads into a burning fireplace when no one was looking. Melanie paid the cashier for the magazine, snacks, and doll.

"Let's roll," Melanie said.

"No one told you to tell my folks about me kissing him, so they had to die," Keith said as they climbed back into the car.

"Look girly-boy, you are killing my high. Where's the food, Mel?" Karen asked.

Melanie handed the bag to Karen as she maneuvered the car through a neighborhood. She turned the headlights off a block away from the destination. She then parked the car along a curb and killed the engine.

The car was filled with the smell of nacho chips and grape soda, and the sounds of snacking. Keith lay in back with his bare feet against the window. Karen had her seat reclined all the way back. Melanie's eyes were fixated on a dark house.

"These are the best chips ever," Karen said.

"These are the best chips in the world," Keith said as he licked his fingers.

"These are the best chips in the galaxy."

"These are the best chips in the universe."

"The galaxy is the universe idiot," Karen said as she turned to face Keith.

"No it's not, you dumb blonde. The galaxy is in the universe," Keith said.

"Shh. Would you both shut up for a second?" Melanie said softly.

Karen and Keith looked at each other and giggled.

Melanie rolled up the drawing, opened the car door and got out, gently closing it behind her. Karen and Keith sat up and watched Melanie tiptoe across the street. Melanie's heart was racing, her ears on high alert. Her eyes were set on the target, the door of Tiffany's house, as she cut across the lawn. She placed the loosely rolled drawing at the bottom of the front door and moved stealthily back to the car. She got in and quietly watched the house for a moment.

"What a creeper," Keith said as he looked at Melanie in the rearview mirror. Melanie did not reply. She just stared back at him through the rearview mirror. Keith returned to snacking on the chips.

"What a stalker," Karen said as she too started crunching.

Melanie did not respond. She started the engine and pulled away from the curb. She turned the headlights on when they were a block away from Tiffany's house.

Chapter Two

The girl's locker room at Henry High School was filled with the varsity girls' track team. The girls rushed to get their clothes changed so they would not be late to the track. The head coach, Mrs. Laughlin, was impatient. Melanie, captain of the sprint team, dressed as quickly as she could. Tiffany and her best friend, Vera, finished changing and walked out the locker room doors into the blinding sunlight. They began a slow jog to the track. Melanie followed, observing the slight movement of Tiffany's blue shorts with orange trim as she jogged, imagining what lay beneath. Melanie inhaled the peach-scented body spray that drifted from Tiffany and Vera. She enjoyed the view and the fragrance.

When they reached the track, they began stretching. Melanie heard a whistle. She looked up and saw Keith sitting in the bleachers, next to a man she didn't know. Keith waved, and Melanie waved back. Keith always attended Melanie's practices. Melanie suspected he really wanted to see the boys' track team in action, but he insisted he was there to support her.

Melanie was stretching her shoulders when she overheard Vera mention Tiffany's latest gift from the secret admirer.

"The drawing was nice," Vera said.

"It was pretty good, wasn't it? I wish I knew who it was," Tiffany said.

"Maybe it was Michael."

"Yeah right. That boy doesn't have a romantic bone in his body."

Melanie smiled when Tiffany called the gesture romantic.

"Hey, you never know. Michael might be surprising you. Why don't you just ask?"

"Ah, so what if I asked and he says no, then what? He will end up accusing me of doing things to make some guy leave me drawings."

"Yeah, I can see him getting a little psycho over that," Vera said.

Coach Laughlin walked over to Melanie and asked, "Will you be starting the warm-up in this century, Melanie?"

Melanie looked up at the six-foot tall, middle-aged woman, and replied yes.

"Come on ladies, let's get this practice going!" Melanie shouted to her team. She led everyone in a series of upper and lower body stretches. Melanie watched Tiffany from the corner of her eye. *She is so flexible,* she thought and then smiled with the thoughts that followed.

After a few stretches, they headed to the track to jog a few laps. Then the varsity boys' team arrived at the track, with Michael in tow. Melanie was about one hundred meters behind Tiffany when she saw her stop jogging. Tiffany then walked over to Michael to give him a hug and kiss. Melanie took note of how their brown skin seemed to melt into one another. The sight made Melanie look down at her own bi-racial lightskin. She felt her heart sink when she thought about how pale and insignificant she would look if she were that close to Tiffany.

"Keep moving, Tiffany!" Melanie shouted as she jogged passed them.

She heard Tiffany say, "Duty calls," as she parted ways with Michael. He proceeded to listen to his coach and captain talk about the not-so-stellar performance the team had at their last meet.

Coach Laughlin told Melanie what she wanted everyone to work on, and Melanie passed it along to the team. The team broke off into three groups--dash, relay, and field.

Melanie gathered the relay team that included Tiffany and Vera. She told them how the coach wanted them to improve their hand-offs.

"Well, someone needs to improve that hair. Looks like a damn bush," Vera said softly to Tiffany, but loud enough so that Melanie could hear.

"You have a problem, Vera?" Melanie asked, looking squarely into Vera's eyes.

Vera looked away. "No," she replied as she shook her head quickly.

Practice continued without another remark from Vera.

Keith and the stranger walked down to the field once Melanie said her goodbyes to her teammates.

"You look like a sweaty mess," Keith said.

"Don't start with me. I am tired as hell," Melanie replied. She fixed her eyes on the man standing next to Keith. She looked over his non-descript brown flip flops, loose jeans and white linen shirt. He wore a feeble expression. "So who's your friend?" she asked.

"Oh, this is Jake. He's a new friend. That Rome guy is in town. Karen wants us all to hang out so we can meet him," Keith said, as the three walked through the school's parking lot.

"I'm down as long as she is paying, because I am a broke joke. She should be wrapping up cheerleading practice now," Melanie said.

"Are they in the gym?" Keith asked.

"Yeah, they should be there," Melanie replied.

"I'll go and get the details," Keith said.

"Oh, I don't do high schools. Bad memories," Jake said with a wince, as the trio approached the school's doors.

Melanie looked at him, puzzled.

"Here, how about you pull the car to these doors and, we'll be out in about fifteen minutes," Keith said, handing Jake the keys.

Jake turned around and headed to the car.

"He doesn't do high schools?" Melanie asked.

"Your closeted ass wouldn't understand," Keith said.

Melanie quickly washed at one of the sinks in the locker room. She was standing at her locker changing her clothes when she overheard Tiffany and Vera talking on the opposite side of the lockers.

"Why do you have beef with her? What did she ever do to you?" Tiffany asked.

"Nothing, it's just that there is something about her that's odd. I mean, come on, she looks like a dude. Don't you think so?" Vera said.

"Melanie does look a little boyish, but I don't think that is enough to not like someone," Tiffany said.

"If she was a guy it would make better sense," Vera said without thinking first.

"What would make sense?" Tiffany asked.

Melanie slowed her breathing so she could fully hear Vera's response.

"Nothing," Vera said quickly.

Melanie felt a warm sensation in the pit of her stomach. "You don't make sense, girl," Tiffany said. Melanie heard them close their lockers and walk away.

Chapter Three

Melanie, Keith, and Jake walked into Albert's, the Kansas City landmark barbeque restaurant. They looked around for Karen. Once they saw she was not yet there, they ordered their food and sat at a circular table.

Melanie began eating her fries, staring at Keith and Jake, who sat next to her. She inhaled the spicy and sweet scent of barbeque sauce rising up from her hot beef briskets.

"So are you two dating, or what?" Melanie asked.

The question surprised Jake and made him choke on his strawberry soda.

"No! We are *just* friends," Keith said as he patted Jake's back.

A teary-eyed Jake batted Keith's hand away and said in a husky wet whisper, "I'm okay. Thanks."

"Sorry. I didn't realize that that was a loaded question," Melanie stated.

"Two bottoms can't be together. That would be too...," Keith racked his brain trying to find the right word to use.

Jake chimed in, "Gay. It would be too gay."

"Exactly, it would be way too gay. I need me a macho man," Keith said.

"You couldn't have said it any sooner. Hello, twelve o'clock," Jake said as he ran his fingers through his hair.

Melanie followed Jake's gaze to a tall black man walking through the door. Cornrows formed an intricate design on the top of his head. His medium brown eyes were in striking contrast to his dark brown skin. His muscular arms seemed to throb, vibrating the platinum chain that hung from his neck. A snug white tank hugged his torso and was draped over a large silver belt buckle. Black jeans hung low around his butt.

Melanie saw Karen rush up behind him through the doors, and turned to look back at Keith and Jake. Keith was fanning himself with his hand. Jake had his lips formed in the shape of an anticipated kiss.

Melanie shook her head and said, "That must be Rome."

"He can roam his fine chocolaty ass right next to me," Jake said. Karen and Rome ordered their food and walked over to the table. They sat at the two empty seats between Keith and Melanie.

Karen introduced Rome to her cousins, and Keith introduced Jake.

"So, Rome, where are you from?" Jake asked.

Rome frowned at Jake.

"You a little nosy man, but since you're my girl's people I will tell you I'm from D-town," Rome replied.

"Where is or what is D-town?" Keith asked.

Rome sucked his teeth in exasperation.

What's with the attitude? Melanie thought.

Karen quickly answered for Rome: "Detroit."

Melanie saw Rome stiffen.

"Well what brings you to KC-town?" Melanie asked.

Keith and Karen giggled at Melanie's referral to Kansas City. Rome sucked the meat and sauce off his baby back ribs. He stopped eating when he saw Jake staring at him. Jake did not look away. Rome tilted his head to look at Karen. "What is this? The gigglin' squad?" Rome said sternly. "I'm looking to expand some opportunities here. Relocate my headquarters."

Undeterred by Rome's brusqueness, Melanie said, "I hope your intentions with my cousin are good."

"Don't worry yourself about that," Rome said, looking Melanie in the eyes.

Feeling the heat rising between Melanie and Rome, Karen quickly changed the subject. "Isn't this the best barbeque spot in town?"

Rome broke the stare and looked at Karen.

"Yeah, it's cool," he replied. He stood up and announced that he needed to use the restroom and walked to the back of the restaurant.

"Where did you find that rat?" Melanie asked.

"He is a nice guy. He's just nervous," Karen said.

"I have to agree with Mel on that one, Karen. Something isn't right with him," Keith chimed in.

"Well, you sure weren't complaining when you were smoking up his weed, now, were you?"

"Oh, so that's how you know him," Melanie said.

"He was with my usual guy and we just started talking. He was leaving the night we met and we just kept in contact over the phone."

"Well, I hope you haven't done anything with him," Keith said.

Jake excused himself to use the restroom.

"No. I am not some whore," Karen whispered.

"Good!" Melanie and Keith said in unison. Then "Jinks!"

The three of them laughed.

"So who's *your* friend?" Karen asked Keith.

"Just a guy I met at a club. We are *just* friends. He is a bottom and plus," Keith looked around and whispered, "He's a bug-chaser."

"A what chaser?" Melanie asked.

"A bug-chaser. You know, has sex without condoms in hopes of getting HIV so he won't have to worry about it," Keith explained.

"Oh, wow. Does he have it?" Karen asked.

"Most likely."

Keith's answer sent a chill down Melanie's spine.

"You get yourself checked, right?" Melanie asked.

"I've only been with one person and it was the first for both of us. But yeah, I verified six months later, I'm negative. The HIV thing gives me the creeps. I've pledged to myself to stay celibate until I find my one and only. I hope you two do the same. Oh but wait I forgot that Melanie is a...virgin," Keith said with a coy smile.

"I get checked. It is scary every time I go back for the results though. But I'd rather know than not know," Karen said.

"Well hopefully my virgin status will change once I get Tiffany away from Michael," Melanie said.

"And how do you think you're going to do that? I don't think dropping off drawings of her is going to do it," Keith said.

"I know. I just have to find a way to divide and conquer," Melanie said.

Karen's eyes lit up when Rome returned to the table.

"Hey baby. I gotta run and take care of something," he said to Karen.

Karen looked disappointed. "Okay."

He left his mostly uneaten food at the table and walked out the restaurant.

Jake sauntered back to the table and asked, "Where did sexy go?"

"The *rat* left," Melanie quipped.

Jake noticed Karen's sad expression. He sat quietly for a moment then said, "Rats like to nibble in restrooms," he paused for a moment.

The solemn look on Jake's face gave Melanie a sinking feeling.

Jake continued in a soft tone, "And once they get a taste they sometimes come back for more." Jake gently slid a piece of paper towards Karen with a number written on it.

Tears formed in Karen's eyes when she saw it was Rome's cell phone number, in his own handwriting.

Chapter Four

Melanie sat in her backyard alone. She listened to the sounds of the crickets and sighed. All the things that were happening around her swirled in her head. Karen and Rome. Rome and Jake. Tiffany and Michael.

Melanie tried hard to focus on Tiffany, but was interrupted by the memory of Karen's watery blue eyes after she found out about Rome's leanings towards the same-sex. Melanie was grateful that Karen hadn't gone any farther with Rome. Especially knowing that he was flirting with Jake the bug-chaser. *Karen really dodged a bullet there,* she thought.

She began to wonder how many men out there were secretly gay or bi-sexual. She even wondered about her dad, but concluded that he couldn't be, since she couldn't remember him ever giving a sign, and she certainly would have noticed.

Melanie then turned her attention to herself. She knew people suspected that she was a lesbian because of her preference for wearing men's clothing, the heavy way she walked, and how she talked about other women. Most people, including her parents, could tell she was sexually attracted to women. Although Melanie's parents suspected, they never approached her about it. They had decided that they would love her just the same, and would allow her to come to them at her own pace and time.

Melanie looked at the skin color of her arm in the moonlight, and thought about her parents. She had had difficulties, being bi-racial. The challenges started with the white kids in elementary school, asking about her hair as they stroked it without permission. Once, Karen called Melanie's father a nigger in front of their classmates. Now, in high school, the black kids would make jokes about the "yellow-lezzy".

Sometimes, she wished that she was born a dark-skinned boy. Then she would be the same color as Tiffany. When they hugged, she could watch their skin melt into one. She wished that when she walked into a place she could hear someone refer to her as "fine chocolaty ass," as Jake had about Rome.

Why couldn't my dad have found a beautiful black woman to hook up with? Melanie thought. She then felt badly for thinking it, because she loved her mom. Melanie never knew her father's side of the family, since they pushed him away when Charles got engaged to Sonja.

Melanie flicked the skin on her arm, as if to flick the color off and then gave a big sigh. She felt trapped between black and white. She also felt trapped by being a female that desired the sexual touch and intimate closeness of another woman. She remembered how Keith had taken matters into his own hands when he beheaded Karen's dolls. The incident made Karen think twice about the way she treated people. Melanie thought about Rome's deception.

In the murkiness of the night and her own feelings, Melanie started making a plan to make Tiffany hers.

Chapter Five

A week later, Melanie, Karen, and Keith were sitting in Karen's smoked-filled basement. Karen was sitting on the floor with a pen in one hand and a joint in the other. She took a hit and passed it to Keith, who was sitting in a club chair.

Melanie was sitting on the couch next to Karen. "Okay read the letter back to me," Melanie said.

Karen cleared her throat and read:

> *Dear Tiffany,*
>
> *You don't know me but I know you. You are the bitch that's been sleeping with my man Michael. We have been together for a year now and I am getting sick and tired of you messing with what is mine! Leave him alone. You better watch your back. Consider this your first and final warning!*
>
> *Yours truly,*
>
> *The bitch that's gonna kick your ass.*

"You should add a P.S. that will really hit it in," Keith suggested. He took a couple of hits from the joint. He skipped Melanie and passed it to Karen.

Melanie thought for a few seconds. "Okay add this: *P.S. You have me to thank for his juicy lips. I provide plenty of moisture thanks to his exploration of my tender parts.*"

"That's good!" Keith exclaimed.

Karen wrote the final words then folded the letter in an origami styled square.

"Are you sure you want to do this?" Karen asked.

"Yes, I am sure. I will be the shoulder that Tiffany cries on when she and Michael break up. I thought this through, and this is what I want to do. So, whatever happened to rat-boy and the bug-chaser?" Melanie asked.

"Jake told me that a couple of nights after the tease in the restroom that Rome came over and hit it," Keith said.

"I would have never guessed that he was that way," Karen said, "Did he at least use a condom?"

"Nope. Jake suggested that he put one on but Rome said that he 'ain't a faggot' and smacked the jimmy from his hand."

"Did Jake tell him about his bug-chasing ways?" Melanie asked.

"He only tells when he is asked. Jake says life is all about choices and he chooses to let others decide their own destiny."

"Wow, that is some fucked-up shit," Melanie said.

"Has Rome tried calling since then?" Keith asked Karen.

"No, I haven't heard from him since he left the restaurant. Good riddance," Karen said.

Chapter Six

The next morning Melanie and Karen walked into the school. Karen had the note in her hand.

"Which locker is hers?" Karen asked.

"Here, I'll show you," Melanie replied.

They walked silently through the large hall filled with students and teachers moving about.

"There it is. Number two thirty-six."

"Okay, I see it. So I'll stick it in the vent slot during first period. I'll get a pass to use the restroom at 9:30. Look for me outside your classroom door and I'll give you a thumb up for success or a thumb down for failure."

"Oh, it better be a thumb up," Melanie said.

The bell rang and they headed to their classes.

Melanie couldn't keep her eyes off of the clock. At 9:00, the math teacher was lecturing about the Pythagorean Theorem. At 9:15, he was demonstrating how the theorem is used. At 9:29, the teacher asked a distracted Melanie to describe the theorem.

"Huh?" Melanie said.

"I asked you to describe the Pythagorean Theorem," the teacher reiterated.

Melanie's eyes were fixated on the door. The clock struck 9:30. *Where is she?* Melanie thought.

"Oh, uhm," Melanie mumbled.

The teacher followed Melanie's eyes to the door. He walked over to the door and closed it. Melanie pursed her lips.

"Please pay attention," the teacher said and then continued his lecture.

The bell rang, finally, at the end of first period. Melanie scrambled to the door to find Karen. She went to Karen's second period class and waited as long as she could before she had to head to class. There was no sign of her. Melanie made her way to her English class and sat down. *Where the heck is she? What happened?* Melanie thought.

Time dragged. Melanie could no longer take the suspense. She raised her hand.

"Yes, Melanie?" Ms. Johnson said.

"Can I use the restroom?" Melanie asked.

"Yes, you *may* use the restroom," she replied.

The teacher handed Melanie a hall pass. Melanie quickly made her way to Karen's class and saw her, nodding in and out of sleep along with a couple of other students.

Melanie positioned herself at the side of the door so that the teacher couldn't see her. She caught the attention of one of Karen's male classmates. The student squinted his eyes to figure out what Melanie was saying. She mouthed Karen's name to him. He mouthed back the word okay. He stopped in mid-turn and his face fell. His head moved slowly across the room to the door. Karen's teacher appeared in front of the door, blocking Melanie's view of the boy and Karen.

"May I help you with something," the tall grey-haired man asked.

"Uhm, yeah I need to talk to my cousin Karen," Melanie replied.

"Is it an emergency?"

"Uh, yes. Yes it is," Melanie replied.

Her hesitation raised doubts for the teacher.

"I'm sure it can wait until later," he said, and then retreated back into the classroom, closing the door behind him.

Melanie finally saw Karen between second and third period. She ran towards her down the hall.

"Hey! No running in the halls," the principle shouted.

Melanie slowed to a fast walk.

"Man cuz, you need to pay attention to the door more," Melanie said.

"Hey, if your teacher didn't close the door you would have had your answer a long time ago. I heard your dumb ass was outside my classroom," Karen quipped back.

"Well, did you do it?"

"Yes. I did it."

"Did anyone see you?"

"No. I was the only one in the hall."

"Cool. Good job," Melanie said in a cheerful voice.

The bell rang. Melanie and Karen headed to their next class.

Later that day, Melanie noticed that Tiffany wasn't at track practice. Melanie spotted Vera and walked up to her.

"Hey, is Tiffany coming to practice?" Melanie asked.

Vera looked at Melanie for a moment before responding.

"No. She isn't feeling very well," Vera replied.

"Is it something serious?"

"Nothing that you should concern yourself with," Vera replied coldly and walked away.

Melanie looked up into the stands and saw Keith sitting alone in the bleachers. She waved him down.

"What's up?" Keith asked.

"I don't have a very good feeling about this. Tiffany isn't coming to practice because she isn't feeling good, according to Vera," Melanie said.

Keith noted the worried look on his cousin's face.

"She's probably just in shock. Remember what you said. You are going to be the shoulder she cries on. That's the plan, right?" Keith asked.

Melanie gave a less-than-confident nod. She looked over at the boys' track team and saw Michael. He looked angry. *What the hell did I do?* Melanie thought.

She regretted writing the letter. Word spread about the letter during practice. People were saying that Michael had been cheating on Tiffany for a year. One person said that the other girl was pregnant and went to a rival school. Another said that Michael had also gotten Tiffany pregnant.

Melanie and Karen walked out the school doors after leaving the locker room. They climbed into a waiting car with Keith behind the wheel, listening to Oasis's "Wonderwall" on the radio.

"I thought that this is what you wanted all along. Why are you looking so glum?" Karen asked Melanie.

"Not like this, especially, not if Tiffany's pregnant. It wasn't part of the plan for me to feel this way. Maybe I should have just continued with the drawings," Melanie said.

"It's most likely that it's just a rumor. Just as how people were saying that the person who wrote it is pregnant. You're not pregnant are you?" Karen said.

"No. Well, technically you wrote while I dictated. So, are you pregnant?" Melanie said, trying to sound jovial.

"Not that I know of!" Karen said.

Keith looked at Melanie in his rearview mirror.

"Maybe you should have just told her how you felt. Or maybe you should have just given the drawings to her yourself, instead of creeping around in the dark like a stalker."

"I don't know. Well, actually, what I know is that I am leaving that whole situation alone. We'll write another letter saying it was a joke or something," Melanie said.

"So, all that for nothing," Keith said as he pulled away from the curb.

Karen shook her head but didn't say anything.

Life is all about choices, Melanie thought.

Yearning

Adrianna

Chapter One

Adrianna woke up to the familiar sounds of her father's bed squeaking. She slowly opened her eyes, which were softly slanted, and squinted at her nightstand. She stretched out one of her long slender arms to reach for the portable CD player on the table. Adrianna placed the headphones on her ears and pressed "play". Listening to Minnie Riperton's "Loving You", Adrianna closed her eyes. She inhaled, then exhaled, fantasizing about having a picnic with her dream man. Her dream man was a person she had never met. His personality and habits were a collection of traits that she created so that he would be the total opposite of her father: thoughtful and attentive. He always asked how her day was and always listened. In turn, Adrianna would do special things for him, like make him lunch and have a picnic at one of their favorite parks in Lincoln, Nebraska.

When the song ended, Adrianna got out of bed. She no longer heard the squeaks of her father's bed. Instead she heard the voice of an unfamiliar woman, who was behind Adrianna's closed bedroom door.

"I had a wonderful time with you, Darren," the woman said to Adrianna's father.

"And I had a *wonderful* time with you this morning," Darren replied. He let out a chuckle that sent shivers down Adrianna's spine. It was the chuckle she knew he gave when he was thinking of something devious.

Darren and the woman's voice wandered past Adrianna's bedroom door, down the stairs and out the front door. Adrianna then heard her father's footsteps come back up the stairs and stop at her door. He knocked at her door gently.

"Baby girl. You up?" Darren said softly.

Adrianna walked over to the door and opened it. Darren looked at his daughter. She was a replica of her mother. She was slender with the same black eyes that Darren had fallen in love with. Her silky straight black hair draped loosely around her shoulders. The only differences were that Adrianna's skin-tone was darker and she was a few inches taller than her mother.

"Good morning, baby," Darren said.

"Good morning Dad," Adrianna replied, looking at a small box that was in his hand.

"Looks like you got something from Mia," Darren said as he handed the box to Adrianna.

Darren married Mia after her mother, Bik, passed away in a car accident. Mia had been Bik's best friend. Mia and Darren divorced shortly before their first anniversary.

Mia had grown tired of Darren's wondering eye. She also grew tired of finding empty condom wrappers in his car, particularly since she never spent time in there with him, in that manner.

Mia had since moved to Minneapolis but she kept in constant contact with Adrianna through email and phone calls, which Adrianna enjoyed. When she got a job offer there, Mia had tried to persuade Darren to allow her to take Adrianna to Minneapolis. Darren refused. Adrianna hoped one day to join Mia in Minneapolis after she was out of high school.

Darren gave Adrianna most of the material things she wanted. But she did not like his philandering ways. Darren seemed to have a new woman leaving the house in the morning on a monthly basis.

Each woman thought she would be his one and only, until Darren caught sight of another who was better than the last. Darren tried to get his women out of the house before Adrianna woke up, but there were times when Adrianna would bump into them when she went downstairs for a midnight snack.

Adrianna took the box from Darren.

"Thanks, Dad," Adrianna said.

"Hey, you want to head over to the Haymarket for a bite to eat with me, around 11:00?"

"Sure."

Darren walked back into his bedroom and Adrianna closed her door.

Adrianna enjoyed the Haymarket district. She liked it most when the stores and restaurants in the area were filled with students from the University of Nebraska. Some of them were people from parts of the world that Adrianna had never heard of. The diversity gave Adrianna comfort that there could be something better than her life in Lincoln.

She sat on her bed and opened the box. Adrianna reached in and pulled out a cedar trinket box with a lacquered purple prairie clover painted on the top. Her face lit up with delight. Adrianna lifted the lid and the scent of cedar rose from the box. A handwritten note was inside. Mia wrote:

Hey honey,

This is a little something that I picked up at a gift shop near the Canadian border in a city called Grand Marais. I thought of you when I saw it. I hope you like it.

Love,

Mia

The thoughtfulness of the gift gave Adrianna a boost. She placed the box on her dresser. She then wrote Mia an email thanking her. Adrianna got ready to go out with her father.

Chapter Two

Adrianna's pale green maxi dress lightly wrapped around her ankles as she and her father walked along the sparsely crowded streets of the Haymarket district, looking for a place that suited both of them. She had adorned her hair with a clip that contained a pink silk gerbera daisy, and wore dark sunglasses.

Darren felt his stomach begin to rumble and placed his hand on his white linen shirt

"Oh, baby girl. We need to decide what we want to do. My stomach is on fire," Darren said.

Adrianna looked around.

"How about there?" Adrianna pointed to a French restaurant.

"There looks great," Darren replied.

Darren dug into his Belgian waffle and began eating. He sipped his mimosa before swallowing all of his food. Adrianna was amused by Darren's reckless abandon when it came to eating. It was the only time when he was in public view that he didn't try to impress a woman. Adrianna delicately ate her fruit salad. She saw a middle-aged woman approach their table.

"Excuse me. Sorry to interrupt, the stranger said. "I just had to stop and say that you are probably the most beautiful creature that I have ever seen. May I ask your ethnicity?" She was sharply dressed in a black pantsuit and hovered over Darren and Adrianna's table. Darren stopped eating while Adrianna replied.

"Thank you for the compliment. I am African-American and Chinese," Adrianna said sweetly.

"Have you done any modeling?" the woman continued.

"No, I haven't."

"Would you ever consider it?"

"No. I have been asked before but I don't have the desire."

"Well, if you change your mind." The woman handed Adrianna her business card. She was an agent at a Chicago-based modeling agency. "Sorry again for interrupting," the woman said, and walked away.

Darren looked at his daughter with a warm smile.

"You know how many girls would kill to be in your shoes? You get all these offers and you just say no, so nonchalantly."

"I want to do something greater with my life."

"Like what?"

"Well this is my last summer of being in high school, you know. I want to do something amazing with my life when I am done. Something like feed the starving children, find world peace..." Adrianna stopped when she saw Darren's eyes move across the room behind her. She turned to see two blonde women walking to a table. Adrianna sighed. Darren didn't notice that she had stopped talking.

Adrianna looked out the window.

"Dad I am going to head over to the coffee shop across the street. Come get me when you're ready to go."

"All right, baby girl." Darren didn't look at his daughter as she left the restaurant. His eyes were fixated on the blondes.

Adrianna walked into the coffee shop and immediately noticed an unfamiliar song playing from the stereo speakers because of its haunting sound. A dark-brown woman sporting curly black hair with tips of golden bronze greeted Adrianna from behind the cash register.

"Hi. May I help you?" the woman asked with a smile, revealing a row of perfectly straight white teeth.

"Uhm yeah. Can I get a medium Italian soda with shots of almond and hazelnut and a peanut butter cookie?"

"Of course you can," the woman said as she began to prepare Adrianna's beverage. "So how are you doing?" the woman asked.

Crappy because I have a slutty dad, Adrianna thought

"Good. Say, what's the song that is playing right now?"

"It's Massive Attack's "Black Milk." You like?"

"Yeah actually I do. It's different."

"Yeah it's pretty chill. The whole album is butter."

"The album is called *Butter*?"

The woman chuckled, her chuckling made Adrianna feel self-conscious.

"No. My bad, the album is called *Mezzanine* and most of the songs on it are smooth like butter."

The woman handed Adrianna her Italian soda.

"My name is Kim. What's your name?"

"Adrianna."

"A pretty name for a pretty girl. It's nice to meet you Adrianna."

Kim held out her hand and Adrianna shook it.

"It's nice to meet you too, and thank you."

"Do you like poetry?" Kim asked.

"Hmm. Not really I don't understand most of it."

Adrianna sipped her soda, looking behind her to see if anyone was waiting in line. There was no one.

"Well, every Friday night we have open mic night here. Bunch of college kids, professors, and some locals come down and share their words. Although you don't seem to really feel poetry, you should come check it out. You never know, there might be a couple of pieces that move you."

"It sounds interesting. I am going to my best friend's birthday party on Friday. What time does it start?"

"Doors open at 6:30. The show starts at 7:00. Here's a flier."

Adrianna heard the door open behind her. She turned to see Darren walking through the door.

"Hey baby girl, you ready to roll?" Darren asked.

"Yeah," Adrianna replied. She turned to face Kim and said, "Thanks for the flier. I will try and make it out next Friday."

"No problem," Kim said with a smile.

Adrianna turned to walk out the door.

"Hey, don't forget your cookie!" Kim shouted.

Adrianna walked quickly back to the counter and took the cookie.

"Thanks again."

"No problem...again."

Adrianna joined her father at the door. Darren looked back at Kim then whispered to Adrianna, "She needs to put a cap on that nappy head."

Adrianna grimaced at her father's comment. She didn't respond. *You need to put a cap on yours,* Adrianna thought.

Chapter Three

The following Friday, Adrianna and Darren walked up to Molly's house. At the front door was a sign that said that the birthday party was in the backyard. They went to the back and saw the party was in full swing. Darren scanned the crowd for available women.

"Remember, Dad. You had a thing with Molly's mom a few months ago. And she's the one that invited you to come," Adrianna whispered sternly to her father.

"I know, baby girl. No harm in looking," Darren said.

Adrianna spotted Molly and walked over to her best friend. Molly had on Daisy Duke shorts and a red plaid shirt that was tied below her bust, the sleeves rolled up to her elbows. The outfit highlighted her slender and toned physique. Her straight black hair hung together in a low ponytail down to the middle of her back. Molly's lips were covered in a glossy red lipstick, which competed with the glossiness of her hazel eyes.

"Happy nineteenth," Adrianna said to Molly.

"Thanks girl. I can't believe that this is my last year in the teens. Can *you* believe it?"

"No, I can't. So, is your new guy here? His name is Xavier, right?"

"Girl, no! You have got to keep up. Xavier is history. It's Paul now. Thank goodness we cleared that up, because here he comes now!"

Adrianna turned to see a muscular man walking in their direction. Paul kissed Molly, and Adrianna was amazed that none of her lipstick transferred to his lips.

"Paul, I want you to meet my best friend, Adrianna. Adrianna, this is Paul."

"Damn, your friend is fine!" Paul exclaimed, "I should hook you up with one of my boys."

Paul's brazen remark startled Adrianna.

"No, that won't be necessary," Molly said. "None of your friends are good enough for my friend. Why don't you go over there and mingle with the other guys and talk about football or something. I want to spend some time with my friend."

Molly wrapped an arm around Adrianna's shoulder and they walked towards the house. Paul stood and stared at the pair walking away, licking his lips. Adrianna looked past Molly and saw her father staring at her friend. A creepy tingle went down Adrianna's spine and she shivered.

"Are you cold?" Molly asked.

"No, my dad is a pervert. He is over there staring at you."

Molly stopped and looked over at Darren, who had stopped talking to a man standing next to him. She winked at him. Darren sent a dashing smile towards Molly. Molly released a fake giggle.

"Ew, Molly, that's my dad. Remember, the guy that banged your mom!" Adrianna exclaimed in disgust.

"Oh, stop being such a prude. You have to loosen up and stop being so sensitive. Come on, help me bring some burgers from the house so we can throw them on the grill," Molly said as she stepped towards her house. Adrianna glared at her father and mouthed the word gross. Darren shrugged his shoulders as if to say, I can't help it. Adrianna looked away, repulsed. She followed Molly into the house.

Adrianna and Molly walked into the kitchen. Molly opened the refrigerator and retrieved burger patties. Adrianna went to the cupboard to get a glass for water.

"Molly, what you did out there was not cool," Adrianna said.

"Oh, Adrianna, I was just playing around. I didn't mean anything by it."

"*You* might have been playing around, but my dad probably took it serious. You know how he is."

Molly saw how upset Adrianna was. She placed the burgers on the counter and gave Adrianna a hug.

"I'm sorry. I seriously didn't mean anything by it. I know how your dad is and I shouldn't have done that." Molly released Adrianna and looked deeply into her eyes. "Please forgive me."

Adrianna's lips formed a small smile, "I forgive you."

The two friends hugged.

"How about we get these burgers on the grill," Molly said.

"Let's do it," Adrianna said.

Adrianna poured herself a glass of water while Molly retrieved the burgers from the counter. The two walked to the backyard together.

Chapter Four

Later, Adrianna was alone in her house, attempting to get the day's events out of her head. She sat at her vanity and thought about going to the coffee shop, to check out the open mic night. She lifted her mother's favorite perfume, Chanel No. 5, from the table. It was the last bottle of perfume that Bik had bought, and Adrianna had kept it for seven years. Adrianna opened the bottle and inhaled the fragrance.

"Should I go out tonight, Mom?" Adrianna whispered. She felt her mother's presence, urging her to go out and have fun. Adrianna stood up from the vanity and walked into her closet, past her mother's traditional Chinese dresses, to the back where her own dresses hung. She decided on a lavender and yellow print maxi dress.

Adrianna's closet was a sacred place for her. She spent hours in it as a child after her mother died. Adrianna spent the time listening to Bik's audio diaries from when she was a teenager. They were recorded on cassette tapes. Adrianna used to rub her mother's dresses as she listened to the comforting voice.

Adrianna got dressed and sprayed her wrists with Chanel No. 5, from a new bottle. She grabbed her keys and purse and headed to her car.

Adrianna entered the crowded coffee shop and looked towards the counter to see if Kim was there. She wasn't. She then scanned the room to see if she could find a spot to park herself. Adrianna saw a brown hand waving in the air. It was Kim, trying to catch her attention. She was sitting near microphones that had been set up towards the back of the coffee shop. Relieved to see a familiar face, Adrianna walked to Kim, who gave her a warm embrace.

"Adrianna, I am so happy that you decided to come. Hey, this is the love of my life, Susan." Kim lifted her hand to a red-haired woman sitting on a chair talking to a man. Kim tapped Susan's shoulder to get her attention. "Babe I want you to meet a new friend,

Adrianna." Susan turned and stood up with a smile, shaking Adrianna's hand. "And this is my buddy Thaddeus." The man next to Susan stood up with a relaxed smile. He shook Adrianna's hand, a little longer than Susan did.

"It's nice to meet you both," Adrianna said.

Adrianna was initially taken aback by Kim introducing Susan as the 'love of her life,' but she was quickly distracted by the penetrating gaze from Thaddeus. He was attractive. She was drawn to his luminous eyes, slight muscles wrapped in dark brown skin, and goatee that framed his well defined lips. A friendly face.

"Adrianna, why haven't I seen you before?" Thaddeus asked.

Adrianna didn't know how to respond.

"Maybe because she doesn't go to the U. Where do you go to school, honey?" Susan asked.

Susan calling Adrianna honey surprised her because she guessed they were probably about the same age.

"Richmond High," Adrianna replied.

"Jailbait," Kim quipped.

"I'll be eighteen next month," Adrianna said.

"And I will be eighteen in two months," Thaddeus said.

"Uhm, how are you only seventeen and already in college?" Kim asked.

"I graduated from high school early," Thaddeus responded.

"And why am I only finding this out now after a year of kickin' it with you?" Kim asked.

"You never asked," Thaddeus replied lightly.

"Wow. So you are a creative, smart, and fine brotha. If only I was straight. If only." Kim said. Susan teasingly slapped Kim's arm. Kim turned to Susan and said, "Hey, baby, you know I only have eyes for you."

Kim's kind words had made Thaddeus blush. Adrianna's interest in Thaddeus was heightened.

Kim looked at her watch. "Shoot I have to get this show rolling. Adrianna, this seat is for you. I hope you enjoy the show. Thaddeus is good peeps." Kim then took Susan's hand and led her to one of the microphones. The crowd hushed to a low murmur. Kim and Susan began to MC.

"So, what are you majoring in?" Adrianna asked in a soft tone but loud enough for Thaddeus to hear.

"I am majoring in finance."

"What inspired you to go that route?"

"I've always been good at math. Plus I have an interest in the stock market. I am especially interested in the market now, with the boom in tech stocks. If I was only interested in math I would probably be a math major. But since I also have an interest in the stock market I decided to pursue finance. Eventually I hope to become an investment banker."

"Wow, that sounds important."

"It's something. How about you? What do you want to do?"

Adrianna felt silly for not having a plan about her future like Thaddeus did.

"Well, I want to save the world, I guess you can say." Adrianna paused. She saw that Thaddeus's attention was focused on her. "I maybe want to start some sort of foundation to help starving kids. I want to help kids." Adrianna looked into Thaddeus's eyes. They radiated sincerity. *He is really listening to me*, Adrianna thought. Thaddeus encouraged Adrianna by asking questions about what she wanted to do. She continued to reveal her thoughts on how to help make the world a better place for as many people as possible.

Time went by swiftly, as various artists went to and from the microphone. There was laughter for the funny poems, and "whoa's" for the deeper poetry. People fanned themselves during the more sensual piece of spoken art, which closed the show.

"Wow! That was…yeah, uhm…*hot*. Where's my girl?" Kim said jokingly into the microphone. The audience laughed. "Well, I thank you all for coming out tonight. Remember, we do this every Friday. We are open until midnight. So please feel free to stay and relax. Until next time, peace." Kim turned off the microphone and walked over to Adrianna and Thaddeus.

"Did you two enjoy the show?" Kim asked

Adrianna and Thaddeus looked at her, both of them blushing.

"I know," said Kim. "Ya'll weren't paying attention. It's peace though. Thaddeus, did you even notice that you didn't perform tonight?"

"Ah, man! No. I was so wrapped up. Hey, did you even call my name?"

"No, dude. I didn't want to wreck the flow that was going on over here."

Adrianna looked at her watch. "Oh, I need to go," Adrianna said hurriedly. Even though she was almost eighteen, Darren held her curfew of 11:00.

"May I get your number?" Thaddeus asked.

"Can I get your number too?" asked Kim. "Susan and I are throwing a backyard potluck at our apartment next Saturday. You are welcome to come, if you have time."

Adrianna looked at Thaddeus. He had a puppy dog expression on his face, trying to quietly urge her to say yes.

"Sure, and let me get yours as well," Adrianna said.

Thaddeus gave a big smile and Adrianna smiled back.

They all exchanged numbers and said their goodbyes. Adrianna rushed to the door but, before she walked through it, she looked back and saw Thaddeus gleaming at her. His smile sent pleasurable tingles throughout Adrianna's body.

Later that evening, Adrianna lay in bed while thinking of Thaddeus. She began to fantasize about having a picnic with her dream man. This time she replaced the unknown man with Thaddeus. The switch made her smile to herself. She then wondered if Thaddeus would be her first intimate encounter. That thought made her nervous. She shifted her body so that she lay on her left side and shook her head to get the thought out of her mind.

Her thoughts drifted to her father. Adrianna couldn't understand why her father was so apparently addicted to sex. She yearned for the undivided attention that he gave other women.

Adrianna had attempted several times to talk to him about the way she felt. All Darren would say was that he was a man that couldn't help himself. He also explained to Adrianna that because he did what he did didn't mean that all men were like him. Darren told Adrianna that he could spot a man like him a mile away and that she should always bring them home to meet him before things became serious. Adrianna did this a couple of times and both times Darren encouraged her to give him the axe. She did. Adrianna figured it takes a dog to know one. She wondered what her dad's verdict would be with Thaddeus.

The phone rang and interrupted Adrianna's thoughts. She reached over to her night stand and picked up the phone.

"Hello?"

"Hello. May I speak to Adrianna, please?" a man asked in a tense voice.

"This is," Adrianna tried to figure out who was on the other end of the line.

The man's voice relaxed, "Hi, Adrianna, it's me, Thaddeus."

Adrianna shot straight up. Her eyes grew large as she mouthed the words oh my goodness. She felt her body temperature rise. She tried to calm herself and managed to say, "Hey, Thaddeus. How's it going?"

"Good. Very good. Sorry if I bugged you with my phone call. I just wanted to say that it was really nice meeting you."

Adrianna's heart was beating rapidly.

"No, you weren't interrupting anything. So there is no need to apologize. I appreciate you saying that though. It was nice meeting you too."

"I hope you are able to make it to the potluck next weekend."

"I will try and make it."

"That sounds good. Well, I better let you go. I have some studying I need to do in the morning. I just wanted to call and say hey. Well, goodnight Adrianna."

"Goodnight Thaddeus."

Adrianna hung up the phone and slowly drifted comfortably to sleep, on cloud nine.

Chapter Five

The sun was barely above the horizon when Adrianna woke up to the sound of an aerosol can being sprayed, and the sound of frantic rummaging. She slowly sat up in her bed, trying to become fully awake and figure out where the sound was coming from.

She looked over at her door, which was open. She then looked over at her closet and saw that its door was open as well. The sounds were coming from the closet which frightened her a little. She wondered where her father was.

Adrianna looked over to her window and thought about opening and crawling out of it. She slowly got out of bed and tiptoed over to the vanity chair and lifted it up. She started to walk to the door when Darren popped out of her closet with an aerosol can in his right hand. Adrianna let out a yelp.

"What the hell are you doing Dad? You scared the crap out of me."

Darren stood wild-eyed in a pair of black cotton boxers.

"Sorry, baby girl. We have an emergency!" Darren exclaimed.

A worried Adrianna asked, "What kind of an emergency?"

Darren's wild eyes soften a bit as he hesitated with his answer.

"We have lice running around here."

"Lice?"

"Yeah, someone infested our home with lice. They are the private kind. Can you believe it?"

"You mean one of your women gave you crabs? What, one of the blondes from the restaurant?" Adrianna's eyes began to get warm.

Darren's eyes turned sad as he watched his daughter melt emotionally. Soon Adrianna dropped the chair and began sobbing.

"What the fuck is wrong with you?" she shouted at him. "Why are you like this?"Adrianna asked between sobs. "I can't believe you. I can't believe that you were in *my* closet spraying your bug spray on *my* mother's things. Why Dad? Why?"

Adrianna's body was shaking uncontrollably from anger, and disgust.

Darren had no answer for his daughter. He wanted to hug and comfort her but he didn't want to risk passing the lice to her.

"Baby, I am so sorry," Darren managed to say.

Adrianna ignored him. Tears continued to flow heavily from her eyes. She grabbed her mother's perfume, keys, and purse and marched past Darren and outside to her car.

Later, Adrianna's arms were crossed as she looked blankly out of Molly's bedroom window. Molly sat quietly on the edge of her bed, looking at her friend.

"Do you think my dad loves me?" Adrianna said aloud what she kept repeating in her head. "Is he capable of love?" she continued.

Molly continued sitting quietly, feeling anguish for her friend.

Adrianna looked at Molly and said, "I am sorry for bringing all of this drama over here."

"Adrianna, you are welcome here anytime, no matter what," Molly said, and pressed her right hand against her chest.

Adrianna used both hands to wipe her cheeks. She then said, "Do you think your mom will let me stay here for awhile? I checked myself for lice before I got out of my car."

Molly and Adrianna locked eyes and smiled softly at one another. They then chuckled lightly.

Molly got up from her bed and walked over to Adrianna and hugged her.

"Of course she won't mind. You can stay as long as you want," she whispered in her ear.

Chapter Six

Adrianna and Molly drove across downtown Lincoln to get to where Kim's potluck was being held.

"Now, Molly, I need you to stay focused. I need you to pay attention and let me know what you think of this guy."

"Okay, okay. I got it."

Molly checked her makeup in the passenger side vanity mirror. A bowl of pasta salad sat in her lap.

"I will be on my best behavior," Molly said sincerely. "Don't worry about me because I am not looking to replace Paul anytime soon. I think I am going to give myself a break from the dating scene."

Adrianna looked over at Molly and grinned.

Adrianna and Molly walked to the backyard of Kim's apartment complex. The sounds of DJ Krush's "Big City Lover" pumped from a boom box. Adrianna spotted Kim and Susan, who were engrossed in a conversation with a group of people. She pointed them out to Molly.

"I like the vibe of this party. It's very hip," Molly said, bopping her head to the beat of the music.

Adrianna scanned the college-aged crowd. She spotted Thaddeus speaking to a classmate. He looked over and their eyes locked. Thaddeus excused himself and walked swiftly over to Adrianna and Molly. Molly saw her friend's demeanor change in a way that she hadn't seen before. *He might be the one*, Molly thought.

"Adrianna. I am so glad you could make it," Thaddeus said.

"Me too. Thaddeus this is my best friend Molly."

"Oh, the one who had the birthday party, right?"

Adrianna wondered how he knew about Molly's birthday when she didn't tell him. She had only told Kim at the coffee shop. He could have only have heard it from Kim. Adrianna then wondered if the invite to the open mic night was an effort to set them up.

"Yes, she is the one," Adrianna replied.

"It's nice to meet you Molly."

Molly and Thaddeus shook hands. Molly was taken aback by his genuine politeness and his confident demeanor.

"It's nice to meet you too," Molly said. "Adrianna, I see food. I am going to make my way over there and go introduce myself to Kim and Susan. You are in good hands," Molly gave a wink to Adrianna that only she could see. Adrianna and Thaddeus fell into a comfortable conversation.

Molly made her way to the food table with the bowl of pasta salad that she and Adrianna brought. She put it on the table and walked over to the group that Kim and Susan were conversing with. Kim and Susan glanced back at Adrianna and Thaddeus and gave nods of approval.

Aching

Nicole

Chapter One

Nicole stood in front of the bathroom mirror, looking over the zig zag cornrows that her stepmother, Ms. Anne, placed in her hair. Her eyes sparkled in admiration like a pair of black diamonds. She heard the intro to Marvin Gaye and Tammy Terrell's "Your Precious Love" from the stereo in the living room. Nicole began to sway slowly side to side, lightly snapping her fingers. It wasn't the music she would have chosen for herself, as she got ready for the teen dance party, but she enjoyed it nonetheless.

Her stepbrother, Malcolm, walked to the doorway of the bathroom and said, "Hey, you bathroom hog. You look like you're ready." Nicole turned to look at him. "You think I can get in there and get ready too?" he asked.

"Ah. Sure, man. It's all yours."

Malcolm walked in, shaking his head. Nicole walked past him and down the hall of the second-floor apartment to the living room. She saw her father, Marshal, dancing a slow two-step with her stepmother. Nicole backed up and watched them dance. Ms. Anne's head was snuggled under Marshal's chin, her face accented by a contented closed lip smile. Marshal's eyes were closed too, as he inhaled the sweet scent of his wife's coconut hair cream. He held Ms. Anne close to him as if she was a delicate and priceless find. Malcolm walked up beside Nicole and they enjoyed watching their parents dancing together. Nicole never saw her father so happy, not even when he was married to her mother.

Nicole's birth mother, Martha, had left her husband and daughter five years earlier, when Nicole was thirteen years old. Marshal and Martha divorced shortly thereafter, citing irreconcilable differences. Nicole and her father hadn't seen or heard from her since.

Ms. Anne and Malcolm had lived across the street. Nicole and Malcolm often played together. Ms. Anne was laid off around the time of the divorce. She worked as a warehouse supervisor in a distribution center in Detroit, and the company she worked for was bought by another firm.

Ms. Anne picked up various jobs through a temp agency during the day, and went to school at night. Her goal was to become a nurse, since she enjoyed working with and helping people. She also figured the chances of getting laid off were slim if she were a nurse, since people will always get sick and need medical treatment. Marshal worked during the day and offered to watch Malcolm for her in the evenings. Nicole enjoyed cooking. She proudly prepared dinner for the three of them. After dinner, Marshal would set aside a plate for Ms. Anne. He presented it to her when she arrived home. She was smitten, always grateful for the gesture. Malcolm would be in a deep sleep by the time she came to pick him up. So she let him sleep over. Before long, Ms. Anne was sleeping over as well. Marshal and Ms. Anne were married after she graduated and she landed a job at one of Detroit's hospitals as a nurse.

When the song ended, Ms. Anne and Marshal opened their eyes, looked at one another, and kissed. Nicole and Malcolm giggled.

Marshal looked over at them with dreamy eyes and asked, "Are you kids ready to go to this party thing of yours?"

"Yes." Nicole and Malcolm replied in unison.

The four of them walked out of the apartment and into the rays of the setting sun. Marshal got behind the wheel of the car, while Ms. Anne sat in the front passenger seat. Marshal turned his head to face his kids in the back. "You all have your belts on?" Marshal asked.

"Seriously Dad? I'm eighteen," Nicole responded.

"Yeah, and I'm sixteen," Malcolm chimed in.

"Well I'm one-hundred. Do you have your seat belts on?" Marshal reiterated.

They all laughed.

"Yes, we have them on," Malcolm said.

"Good, now let's get you two to this party," Marshal said as he drove away from the curb and headed towards the highway.

"Man, look at this neighborhood," Marshal said flatly. "I really don't see how anything is going to get better around here."

Nicole looked out her window at the decaying neighborhood. Every few houses on a block had boarded-up windows, fallen porches, and overgrown yards. There was the occasional dirty couch sitting on the curb, a cluster of abandoned grocery carts, and deteriorated cars and trucks in driveways.

"This is one raggedy place. I remember when it didn't look like this. Well, I don't remember it fully because I was just a kid then but I do remember it didn't look like this. My dad used to talk about how nice things were when everyone was in their own community and there was pride in that. Sure, black folks had issues when they were working side-by-side with the white folks, but you got to go home with your own people. You'd talk about the bad day then have a block party," Marshal's eyes glistened as he remembered what his father had told him. "Then the jobs started leaving. Things started to shut down. Then the thing happened when the white people started leaving. Oh, what did he call it?" Marshal racked his brain trying to remember the term.

Ms. Anne knew the term but waited a bit for Marshal to remember. When she felt he wasn't going to get it, she answered, "White flight."

"Yeah, baby. White flight. Then my pops gets a visit by a man to buy a house in a place black people didn't live. He talked it up. Made my dad think he was buying into some gold or something. Then…well, you know, look around," Marshal's expression turned grim.

Ms. Anne squeezed Marshal's thigh and said, "Well we don't have to see this anymore now that we are moving to a better neighborhood soon. Just in time for summer. We can have a nice graduation party for Nicole in the backyard."

"And look at pretty houses and yards," Malcolm chimed in.

"Yes, baby. And look at pretty houses and yards," Ms. Anne replied.

Nicole didn't say anything. She just listened and took it all in.

Police officers were standing in front of the club when Marshal pulled up to the curb.

"All right, you two have fun and be safe. We will be back to pick you two up right here in two hours."

"Okay!" Malcolm shouted as he and Nicole scurried out the car.

They got in line and could hear the bass boom from Coolio's "Gangsta's Paradise".

"You think Crystal is going to be here?" Malcolm asked.

"Yes. I am pretty sure of it. I heard her talking to her friends about coming out tonight."

"Do you think Crystal is going to be here with Jerome?"

Nicole looked at her brother and scrunched her face.

Nicole was irritated by the thought of Jerome being inside the club. "Let's hope not," she managed to say.

A bouncer checked their school IDs and allowed them to pass to the next bouncer, who frisked them. He then allowed them to pass to the third bouncer, who ran a hand-held metal detector along their bodies. They were then allowed to enter the club.

Nicole and Malcolm walked over to the bar and she shouted an order of two Shirley Temples to the bartender. They got their drinks and took in the scene. There were girls in Daisy Duke shorts and tank tops tied in knots behind their backs. Some of them had purple and red hair weaved into their naturally black hair. Most of the boys wore basketball jerseys, while others had on blue jeans and t-shirts. They were all dancing and appeared to be having a good time.

"Gangsta's Paradise" gave way to the familiar choo choo intro for Quad City DJ's "C'mon N'Ride It (The Train)". The crowd went wild. Tingles ran up and down Malcolm's spine. "That's my song!" he shouted. He got the dance bug and gave his drink to Nicole then made a beeline to the dance floor, doing The Train. Some kids from school found him and they all danced together. Soon, Malcolm began to outdance them all and a circle formed around him. Nicole watched and enjoyed the song vicariously through Malcolm. She wished she were that carefree.

Nicole heard a familiar voice shout into her right ear, "Whaddup cuz? Holding up the bar I see. That downy sure does know how to dance!"

Nicole looked over and saw her former best friend, Jerome. Standing next to him was Crystal.

Nicole shouted back, "His name is Malcolm and he has Down Syndrome. I am not going to tell you again!"

Jerome shrugged his shoulders.

An irritated Nicole looked at Crystal, who was looking at the dance floor.

"You know, you really need to get in this business thing with me, man," Jerome shouted. "I mean, look at me. I am blowing up!" He flicked the two-carat diamond studs in both ears, smiled to reveal a rack of shiny gold teeth, and stomped his right foot to highlight a brand new pair of Jordans.

"Hey. You know that kind of stuff isn't for me," Nicole replied.

"Yeah, that's right, you going to the U of M or some shit, right? Well holla at your boy when you wake up and realize that shit ain't gonna do a damn thing for ya."

Nicole didn't respond. She just blinked a few times, inhaling deeply. "C'mon N'Ride It (The Train)" gave way to Shaggy's "Boombastic".

"This is my song!" Crystal shouted. She turned to Jerome to get him to dance with her. She ignored Nicole. One of the bouncers came up to Jerome and leaned over to say something in his ear. They walked off. Crystal pouted slightly, and she then walked over to dance with Malcolm, who was still the center of attention. She began to slowly roll her hips, her hands slowly winding above her head in front of Malcolm. Without missing a beat, he began dancing in unison with her. Nicole watched the strobe lights run around Crystal's body. One light would shine on her tightly-woven long black ponytail, while another glittered on her cleavage that was held up by a white halter top. Malcolm held Crystal's waist as they danced. He brought her up when she got too low to the ground, as Malcolm thought someone might get a peek of what she wore underneath her short white skirt.

Some of the boys watching them dance had their hands covering their mouths as they admired Crystal's pretty face and beautiful body. None of them dared to make a move on her, because she was Jerome's girl. The girls were less focused on Crystal and more focused on where Jerome was. Some of them were searching for him in hopes they might be the next princess in Jerome's life.

Jerome walked back to Nicole after dealing with the bouncer. He shouted into Nicole's ear, "Your brother is the only one who can get away with that shit. Let me get in there and show 'em how it's done!"

Nicole smiled. *Malcolm is one lucky guy*, she thought.

Jerome walked over to Malcolm and tapped him on his shoulder. Malcolm released Crystal's waist and Jerome took over. Malcolm walked back to the bar where Nicole stood. He was sweating. Malcolm took his watered down drink from Nicole and gulped it down.

"So, Crystal came tonight with Jerome," Malcolm stated.

Nicole grimaced and replied, "Yup."

Chapter Two

The following Saturday, Nicole woke up in her top bunk to the smell of bacon, eggs, and pancakes. She interlocked her fingers and then stretched her arms. Nicole lay for a moment, listening to Ms. Anne and her father talking warmly with one another in the kitchen. She heard Malcolm stirring below her in the bottom bunk. Nicole propped herself up on her elbows and looked out the bay window. The morning sunlight cast a soft yellow glow on the dusty window. For Nicole, this spring marked the end of being a senior in high school and the beginning of adulthood. She climbed down and went to the bathroom to wash up for breakfast. She was soon followed by Malcolm.

"Has anyone picked up the mail yet today?" Nicole asked. She pulled out a chair at the dining room table. Ms. Anne placed food on a plate in front of her.

"You know the mail doesn't run this early, champ," her father replied.

"I just can't wait to see if I got into the U," Nicole stated.

"I'm sure you did, baby," said Ms. Anne. "They would be fools to not accept you. You can show them a thing or two with your good grades and the good work you've done around this neighborhood."

"Have you decided yet if you are going to live here, or stay on campus?" Malcolm asked.

"It all depends on what scholarship I get. I would like to live on my own. Well...I will most likely be living with roommates, but I still will be on my own."

"I think that you should continue to live here and then just drive to school each day. Plus, your job is here," Malcolm said as he placed a chunk of pancake in his mouth.

Nicole's heart skipped a few beats as she looked at Malcolm who was looking down at his food while he chewed. The thought of not being in close proximity to him, to watch and protect him made her feel anxious.

"I will just be in Ann Arbor. That's only thirty minutes from here. There will also be plenty of gas stations there for me to work at."

The conversation was halted by the familiar slam of the postman's truck door. Nicole pushed her chair out and ran to the window to confirm. "It's him!" she shouted when she saw the white truck parked on the street below. She ran out the apartment and down the stairs.

"Hey Nicole," the postman said as he began to shuffle through the mail looking for the envelope he knew Nicole was racing to see.

"Has it come yet?" Nicole asked with wide eyes.

"It doesn't look like it, sweetie," the postman said. He handed her the mail for her family. She thanked him and turned to walk back upstairs, when she saw Crystal walking alone in front of the mail truck. Nicole walked outside and said hi.

"Hey, Nikki," Crystal said with a smile.

"Oh, so now you know my name. You weren't trying to say anything to me a week ago," Nicole said.

"I know. You know how Jerome be thinking things."

"Where is the king?" Nicole asked sarcastically, looking around.

"Out of town. He should be back later tonight."

"Where did he go?"

"He went down to Kansas City to look into some opportunities."

"Opportunities, huh?"

"Don't start, Nikki. What else is there to do for a young black man in America."

"Plenty. He's just being lazy. Anyway, I don't want to talk about him. You want to come up and have breakfast?"

"Did Ms. Anne cook?"

"Yes," Nicole said with a proud smile.

"Then count me in!"

Chapter Three

"Ms. Anne, you are the best cook in the neighborhood. Thank you for letting me join you all this morning for breakfast," Crystal said.

"You're welcome, baby. You are welcomed here anytime," Ms. Anne replied.

Marshal noticed the affectionate gaze Nicole gave Crystal. He rubbed the back of his head. It pained him to see his daughter carry deep feelings for someone that he knew she had no future with. *She has to learn on her own. Just as I did with her mother,* Marshal thought.

"So what do you have planned this weekend, Crystal?" Marshal asked.

"Not much. My mom is over in Windsor with her new boyfriend. Jerome is down in Kansas City on business."

"Oh, Jerome is on a *business* trip," Marshal said.

"Dad, please don't go there," Nicole said delicately to her father.

Marshal studied Crystal for a moment.

"He isn't as bad a person as people like to make him out to be. Nikki, you should know that. After all, you two used to be best friends."

"Yeah, that was back before he started selling drugs to my other friends, and the mothers of my friends."

Crystal didn't respond. Instead her eyes turned sad and she slowly sucked in the corner of her bottom lip, biting on it softly.

"Today is such a beautiful day," said Ms. Anne cheerfully. "Nicole, maybe you and Crystal should take my car and head to the beach at Lake St. Clair."

Marshal cringed on the inside at the thought of Nicole alone with Crystal. He hoped his daughter was as smart as he thought she was.

"I wanna go too," Malcolm said.

"No. I want you to stay here with us. Have some quality time with your parents," Ms. Anne said.

Malcolm was not pleased with his mother's suggestion, but he saw Nicole's mood brighten at the thought of spending the day alone with Crystal. He agreed to stay home.

"So, what do you think, Crystal? Would you like to join me at the beach?"

"That does sound nice. I've never been there before. Is it far from here?"

"No, not all. It's just up 94," Nicole replied.

"Can you give me an hour to run home and change?"

"Absolutely!" Nicole said ecstatically.

"I will pack you two a lunch to take with you," Ms. Anne said.

Nicole and Crystal thanked Ms. Anne. Crystal left to change her clothes and Nicole went into her bedroom to get ready for the big day.

Chapter Four

Nicole enjoyed maneuvering the car through traffic with Crystal by her side. She wasn't sure how to position her body. She thought about slouching to her left side with her left hand under her chin while the right hand gripped the steering wheel. She then thought about leaning to her right while cupping Crystal's left hand like she saw her dad do with Ms. Anne. Nicole ended up settling for her left hand on the steering wheel while her right hand cupped the knob of the stick shift.

Crystal wore a coral-colored sundress. From the corner of her eyes, Nicole soaked in the way the dress laid delicately on top of Crystal's legs, just above her knees. Nicole felt her body temperature rising. She coolly switched hands on the steering wheel. Her left elbow rested on the bottom of the window while her left index finger caressed the bottom of her lip.

"I am really excited about going to the lake. I've heard about how pretty it is," Crystal said. She looked over at Nicole, admiring Nicole's cornrows, high cheekbones, and brilliant black eyes. Crystal was drawn to Nicole's androgynous appearance. Her mind began to wonder about what she might look like without any clothing.

"You won't be disappointed. I am happy that you are going for the first time with me."

"I am happy that I am going for the first time with you too."

Nicole and Crystal locked eyes and they both felt intense warm tingles radiating through their bodies. Nicole looked away quickly and tried to focus on the road.

The beach was packed with people taking advantage of the hot spring day. Kayakers glided across the lake while children splashed in the water. Tanning oil glistened on women in bikinis laying on beach towels, while seagulls walked around looking for food. A breeze carried the scent of barbecue from the grills near the boardwalk as

Nicole and Crystal walked through the grass to an empty picnic table. Nicole watched Crystal as they walked, trying to gauge whether or not she liked what she saw.

"So, what's the verdict?" Nicole asked as they sat down at the picnic table.

"It is wonderful," Crystal said, beaming at Nicole.

"Yes it is," Nicole replied, looking intently at Crystal.

Crystal began to blush.

"Crystal, can I ask you something," Nicole couldn't believe the words leaving her lips.

"Sure."

Nicole tried to think of something else to ask, but drew a blank, so she said what was on her mind.

"Could you ever see yourself with a person like me," Nicole asked hesitantly.

"You mean could I ever see myself with *you*, right?"

"Yeah."

Crystal didn't answer right away. Instead she looked away, at a man playing in the water with his two black Labrador Retrievers.

Without looking at Nicole, Crystal said, "Jerome and I are moving to Kansas City soon after he gets back."

Nicole was stunned. Her heart sank.

Crystal felt the shift in Nicole's energy and turned to face her. "I wanna go play in the water."

"Did you bring a swimsuit?"

"No."

Crystal stood up and ran towards the beach before Nicole could say anything else. Nicole followed, with a heavy heart. Crystal kicked off her shoes and began inching slowly into the lake when Nicole caught up to her.

"It's colder than I thought it would be," Crystal said.

Nicole rolled her pants up to her knees and waded in next to Crystal. They stopped when the water reached their knees. Crystal scooped up water and splashed it in Nicole's face. The sudden coolness snapped Nicole out of her funk. She scooped water and splashed Crystal with it. Soon they were both laughing and splashing each other, enjoying the moment, enjoying each other.

A slightly damp Nicole and Crystal strolled along the boardwalk as the sun began to set.

"I had a really good time with you today," Crystal said.

"Thanks. Me too. I am actually getting hungry."

"Do you think the food Ms. Anne packed for us is still good?"

"Probably not, since it has been sitting in a hot car all day long. Say how about we head over to Birmingham for dinner?"

"Where the rich people live?"

"It's where you and I will find a decent meal."

"Sure. I've never eaten there before."

"This is a day of new experiences."

Crystal looked over at the speedboats and sailboats at the dock.

"Yes, it is. Hey, can we walk over there on the dock and look at the boats on our way back to the car?"

"We can do whatever you want," Nicole said, resisting the urge to hold Crystal's hand.

Chapter Five

A muted maroon glow created ambiance in the Italian restaurant that Nicole chose in Birmingham. The soft murmur from the conversations of the diners swirled in the air, and waiters glided to and from the restaurant's kitchen. The edges of a white tablecloth rested loosely on top of their thighs as Nicole and Crystal waited for a waiter to take their order.

"I hope I don't look crazy after running around in the lake all day," Crystal said.

"You look fine," Nicole responded. Nicole clasped her hands under her chin, watching the flickering candle in the center of the table.

"This place is pretty fancy. How did you find out about it?" Crystal asked.

"My dad took Ms. Anne here for their first date."

So Nicole brought her here because she thought that they were on a date. Crystal was a little uncomfortable with all the undivided attention from Nicole. She wasn't used to someone treating her so well. She didn't feel deserving. Crystal was used to even her mother choosing someone else over her--usually a man. She was used to Jerome's selfish ways and catering to his needs. She wasn't used to someone catering to her needs. She appreciated Nicole's efforts but, still, Crystal didn't feel comfortable. She didn't want to lead Nicole on.

"Well, this is a nice spot for couples. Maybe we should have gone to burger joint or something."

"So you don't want to eat here?"

"I'd rather not."

"Well, okay. Let's get the waiter and let him know we will go someplace else."

Nicole was irritated by Crystal's desire to leave. She gave the waiter a five-dollar bill for his effort and escorted Crystal out of the restaurant.

Nicole and Crystal got back into the car. Nicole didn't start the car right away. Instead she turned to Crystal and asked, "So where would you like to go?"

"Plany's," Crystal replied.

"Plany's, the hole-in-the-wall near downtown Detroit?"

"Hey, hole-in-the-walls have some of the best food."

"I know. I agree. It is just a totally different kind of place."

"We can get some food to-go and some beer and then bring it back to my place."

"I don't drink."

"Well, I can have some beer. I need to get my drink on," Crystal said.

The conversation made Nicole see things in a different light. Nicole began to see something in Crystal that she hadn't seen in the years that she had known her. She saw a person who had different desires than she had. The differences reminded Nicole of her mother and father. Nicole thought about all the years of unhappiness that her mother had, because her desires for a life of luxury were not fulfilled with Marshal. Nicole remembered the numerous times her father attempted to make her mother happy, and how, with each failed effort, he lost a part of himself. Nicole thought back to earlier in the day, when she had heard her father and Ms. Anne warmly conversing while fixing breakfast. She remembered how comfortable they were together the week before, dancing in the living room. Maybe Crystal was not the person for her.

Nicole placed the key in the ignition and started the car.

Chapter Six

The bright lights from Plany's were beaming into the parking lot as Nicole pulled into a spot.

"Plany's, here I come," Crystal said. "I can't wait to get my grub on. I am starving."

Nicole felt her own stomach rumble but didn't say anything. She turned the engine off and got out of the car. Crystal noticed Nicole's silence.

The bright lights in the diner made them narrow their eyes as they walked inside. The line was long to the cashier, not a welcoming sight to Nicole and Crystal who hadn't eaten since breakfast. Marvin Gaye's "I Want You" was playing. The song's lyrics made Nicole shake her head.

"I know this line is long, right," Crystal said, believing Nicole's head shake was about the crowd.

"Yeah, I can't believe it."

The two got in line. Nicole began to sing along to the song in her head, *I want you the right way*. She then turned to Crystal and said, "Crystal, what do you or how do you envision your life in Kansas City?"

Crystal was surprised by Nicole's question but happy that she had initiated a conversation.

"Uhm, well let's see. I always liked kids. So, I see myself having at least two little ones. Two girls would be great because girls mature faster than boys. I can't be taking care of three babies at once. I see me and Jerome in a nice house somewhere in a suburb or something," Crystal said.

"*Three* babies?"

"Nikki, you know Jerome is a big baby," Crystal chuckled.

Nicole smiled and continued singing along with the song in her head, *I want you to want me too, just like I want you*.

The line moved slowly to the cashier.

"What are you going to get?" Crystal asked.

"I'm getting my usual."

"What is your usual?"

"Fried chicken wings, an order of hush puppies, and peach cobbler to top it all off. What are you going to get?"

"Shoot, everything on the menu, the way I'm feeling. I am going to get fried catfish, collard greens, cornbread, and pound cake. Mmm, just thinking about it makes me even hungrier. It also doesn't help that I can smell the food cooking."

"I know that's right."

"I really like your hair, by the way. I was admiring it in the car when we were heading to the lake. Who did them for you?"

"My stepmom hooked me up."

Crystal wasn't sure if she should ask the next question, unsure how Nicole would respond.

"Do you ever miss your mom?"

Nicole coolly replied, "No, I don't. It has been very peaceful since she left."

"Do you ever wonder what she is doing, or how she is doing?"

"No. I can't worry about someone who hasn't reached out to ask about me. Divorcing each other was probably the best decision my parents ever made."

"I thought that having you would have been the best decision that they ever made."

Nicole smiled warmly at Crystal.

"Sure, that could be another one."

"Well, your dad certainly seems to be very happy now."

"I agree. He is with someone who appreciates and loves him for him. He is no longer in Lala Land, trying to make something work with someone who isn't on the same wavelength."

"That's a really good thing," Crystal said.

The line progressed, and Nicole and Crystal took a step forward to the counter. Nicole continued singing along to the song as Crystal gave her order to the cashier, *This one-way love is just a fantasy.*

Chapter Seven

Later that night, Nicole parked her stepmother's car in front of their apartment building and turned on the interior lights. She turned the engine off and looked at Crystal who had food from Plany's resting on her lap.

"Thank you for spending the day with me," Nicole said.

"Thank you for taking me."

"You know, we probably really should be thanking Ms. Anne for the suggestion."

"True," Crystal said with a nod.

Since Crystal was going to be leaving soon, Nicole decided there was no harm in being open and honest.

"I am going to miss you when you leave. We've known each other for what seems to be forever. You know, I always had a crush on you. You have always been the prettiest girl in school. You've also been one of the nicest people in the neighborhood."

Crystal had always known that Nicole had a crush on her.

"I will miss you too, Nikki."

Nicole was surprised that Crystal didn't acknowledge the part about her crush.

"So, when exactly are you guys leaving?"

Crystal paused before answering.

"Next week."

"Next week? What about school?"

"Well, Nikki, I might have been…the prettiest as you said but I haven't been the smartest."

"So, what…you're dropping out of school? What does your mom think about that?"

"Yup, and my mom couldn't care less, as long as she has someone warm to snuggle up with at night."

"Wow, Crystal you sure are full of surprises today."

Nicole was disappointed in Crystal. The feeling surprised her.

"Well, I wish you all the best," Nicole said.

"Thanks. I wish you the best at the U. What are you studying anyways?"

"I haven't been accepted yet. I am just going to take my general studies classes until I can decide what my major should be in."

"I'm sure you will get in and I know that you are going to be great at whatever you do."

Nicole thought about saying a few words to Crystal, to encourage her to choose a different path, but she thought it would be useless. She figured that Crystal was mature enough to know that following a drug dealer to another state wasn't the best thing for her to do.

"Thanks Crystal, that means a lot. Well, I am going to head upstairs."

Crystal and Nicole got out the car. Nicole locked the doors and walked to the sidewalk where Crystal was standing under a lamppost. Crystal gazed into Nicole's eyes, and noticed that their brilliant blackness was fading to an unfamiliar shadow.

"So, I guess this it," Crystal stated.

"Yeah. I think this is it."

Crystal hugged Nicole and then walked across the street to her apartment building. Nicole stood on the sidewalk and watched Crystal climb the stairs to the front door when she heard the familiar boom of a bass. It was Jerome's car, creeping down the street. Crystal turned around and ran down the stairs to the car. Jerome stopped the engine and got out, not even noticing Nicole standing across the street.

"They call me Rome baby!" Jerome exclaimed with his arms wide open anticipating the embrace of Crystal. Crystal dropped the bag of Plany's food and leaped into his arms.

"Who calls you Rome? Why do they call you Rome?" Crystal asked.

"My new associates down in Kansas City, because I'm 'bout to build an empire! Now I've been driving all these miles thinking of one thing."

"What's that?" Crystal asked.

"I want those warm brown thighs wrapped around my waist."

Crystal did a slight leap and wrapped her legs around Jerome's waist. He firmly squeezed her butt then slapped one of her butt cheeks as he carried her up the stairs. Crystal looked across the street at Nicole, watching from under the streetlight. Crystal closed her eyes as Jerome closed the building's door behind them.

Nicole's heart ached for what she knew would never be.

Bye Crystal, Nicole thought.

Chapter Eight

Nicole awakened to Malcolm's oblique-shaped eyes staring at her. He had climbed up to her bunk, waiting for her to wake up.

Malcolm placed his hand on the side of her face and asked, "Nicole, are you depressed?"

Nicole stretched her arms and said, "No, I am not depressed. Just a little sad is all."

"I don't like to see you like this. I like it when you run around with me and laugh. I like it when you smile."

"I will be that way again. I want to lay and think for a little bit."

"Are you hiding from Crystal?"

"Kind of. I am not in the mood to run into her."

"Would it help if you knew that Crystal was leaving right now and that you will never see her again?"

"What do you mean?"

"She and Jerome are packing up his car right now."

Nicole flung her covers off. Malcolm hurried off the bed to allow Nicole to get off. She ran to their bay window. She saw Crystal hauling the last of her belongings to Jerome's car, while he sat on the stairs smoking a cigarette. Nicole sighed.

Jerome extinguished his cigarette once Crystal placed the box in the back seat of his car. She got into the passenger seat and he got into the driver's seat. The sound of bass thundered from his car when he turned the ignition. The car pulled away from the curb, the bass fading.

Nicole sat on the ledge of the bay window and looked at the hardwood floor.

"All done," Malcolm said.

Nicole looked at him. She felt the release of tension in her body, feeling more relaxed with each breath she took. Malcolm saw Nicole come back to life. She smiled.

"Yup, all done," she said with a nod.

They heard the familiar slam of the door of the postman's truck, then the sound of their front door closing. Nicole and Malcolm walked into the living room. Ms. Anne was starting breakfast, but their father was nowhere to be seen.

They heard footsteps racing up the stairs. Marshal came through the front door with the postman behind him. He tossed a few letters on the coffee table but kept one letter in his hand.

"The letter is here!" he exclaimed.

Ms. Anne rushed in from the kitchen.

Nicole's eyes widened, her heart was thumping rapidly. She slowly took the letter from her father. Everyone in the apartment held their breath as she opened the letter.

"Oh my goodness, I'm in!"

About the Author

Ninamaste MaTuri is a Minnesotan who enjoys writing, and hopes to continue writing stories. She also enjoys wine tastings, visiting museums, and traveling, in her spare time. She is author also of *The Preludes*.

You can visit Ninamaste at:
www.ninamastematuri.com